A Book of Poetry

About Inspiration,

Encouragement & Love

By

Farrell J. Curry

Dedication

I dedicate this book to my daughter, Amanda, my treasure from Heaven.

I am so proud of the woman that you have become.

Table of Contents

~ Let not man be exalted

or lifted up but every

good, noble and pure deed

done under Heaven let

God receive the glory

because it has come from

Him ~

Life's Journey

Life is a journey that we take

based on choices that we make.

Through the woods of life,

we go down the paths

that we are shown.

Some choose the easy way

that is clearly seen,

but few choose the way

that has to be walked by faith

and not by sight alone.

"Your word is a lamp unto my feet and a light unto my path."
(Psalms 119:105)

"You will show me the path of life; in Your presence is fullness of joy; At your right hand are pleasures forevermore."
(Psalms 16:11)

"For we walk by faith, not by sight."
(2 Corinthians 5:7)

A Father's Tears

Father's tears are falling.

Another one of His children has strayed

and gone their own way.

He forever watches and beckons.

Come back home child this day,

Come back home to stay.

"And not many days after, the younger son gathered all together, journeyed to a far country, and there wasted his possessions with prodigal living."
(Luke 15:13)

"But when he had spent all, there arose a severe famine in that land, and he began to be in want."
(Luke 15:14)

"And he arose and came to his father. But when he was still a great way off, his father saw him and had compassion, and ran and fell on his neck and kissed him."

(Luke 15:20)

Back Home

I found myself in a wilderness one day,

wandering far from home.

How I got there, I do not know.

Maybe one small step at a time,

away from the way that was known.

I could not see that my feet were

leaving a path that was meant for me.

One that was so plain and so easy to see.

My heart longed for home, a place where I belonged.

I called out to my Savior, and He answered me.

He led me back to the path that I needed to be on.

As we walked together, side by side,

I heard many voices in the distance, the sounds of a choir,

exalting His precious Holy name.

Then, a tall steeple came into view,

one that reached way up to the sky.

It was the house of the Lord,

a house filled with His love, prayer and praises.

His love and warmth filled my soul

as He led me in, and I joined my brothers and sisters to sing

His praises; finally I had made it back, yes back

where I needed to be.

Back on the straight and narrow path

that leads to His house and then finally home.

On the path that was meant for me.

"... let him return unto the Lord, and He will have mercy upon him; and to our God, for He will abundantly pardon."
(Isaiah 55:7)

"Come now, and let us reason together," says the Lord, "Though your sins are like scarlet, they shall be as white as snow; though they are red like crimson, they shall be as wool."
(Isaiah 1:18)

"Create in me a clean heart, O God; and renew a steadfast spirit within me. Restore to me the joy of Your salvation and uphold me by Your generous Spirit."
(Psalm 51:10, 12)

Your First Step

Your first step of faith is never easy,

because it takes courage

when your one of His chosen few.

Just remember He promised to be there,

to help you walk the path

that has been laid out before you.

So, just be bold and courageous,

and step out in faith.

He will be there to meet you and walk with you,

every step of the way.

It is not promised that the road

you have to walk on will be an easy one,

but just remember His grace is sufficient.

He will encourage and strengthen you,

to complete each and every task.

You must choose, however, to remain,

Yes, remain on the straight

and narrow path that He has.

Such blessings and rewards

He has for you.

So many things to show His chosen few.

So, my friend, walk on with courage,

knowing that you're never alone.

Walk on. Walk on.

If you're not on the right path today,

all you have to do is

take your first step to Him.

Take it and He will bring you in to

Life eternal with

Peace and joy that never ends.

"Have I not commanded you? Be strong and of good courage; do not be afraid, nor be dismayed, for the Lord your God is with you wherever you go."

(Joshua 1:9)

"I will instruct you and teach you in the way you should go; I will guide you with My eye."

(Psalms 32:8)

"The steps of a good man are ordered by the Lord, And He delights in his way."

(Psalms 37:23)

The Lighthouse

The storms of life came one day,

like a ship on a stormy wind, tossed sea

I struggled to find my way.

Not Knowing where I was,

not able to see the light of day,

But, then I remembered a night not so long ago

when my ship was tossed to and fro,

not knowing which way to go,

I looked out across the sea

and saw a light in the darkest night.

This light I know was meant for me,

it showed me the way that I should go.

It guided me to shore

and saved me from the jagged rocks below.

In the Safety and Peace of the Harbor

my ship now rests away from the wind,

the night and the stormy sea

that tried to push me on the rocks to kill me.

Yes, I am battered, bruised and torn,

but I am now safe and warm.

I am being repaired to sail another day

on the beautiful sea of life.

To weather another storm maybe,

but I will not be afraid

because I know that there is a Lighthouse

that shines brighter, yes,

brighter than the brightest day.

Jesus is the Lighthouse,

and I will tell the world

how through the darkest night

that light shines for me and for them.

So, if you are in a storm

and the way isn't clear

just remember look to Jesus

and He will draw you near.

He is the Harbor of Safety, Peace and Rest

to those who are in distress.

"The Lord is my light and my salvation; Whom shall I fear?   The Lord is the strength of my life; Of who shall I be afraid."
(Psalms 27:1)

"You shall not be afraid of the terror by night, nor the arrow that flies by day,"
(Psalms 91:5)

"Because you have made the Lord, who is my refuge, Even the Most High, your dwelling place."
(Psalms 91:9)

"You will keep him in perfect peace, Whose mind is stayed on You...."
(Isaiah 26:3)

God gave me The Lighthouse poem when I was in a terrible storm and away from Him. It is one of my favorites. It is not only beautiful but anointed as well. I am so glad that he chose me to write such poetry. Why he chose someone like me, I will never know. I have failed Him many times and yet He still chose to use me proves His undying love for me and you. I hope whoever comes across this poem it will bless, enlighten, and truly find you.

Come Unto Me

The Spirit beckons and calls come unto the Savior,

all who are destitute, hungry and poor.

Stand under His cross and behold

the love He has for you.

Yea stand under the fountain stream of blood,

to wash you clean and make all things new.

Riches beyond all measure are yours.

All of heaven's treasures, peace, love and joy

are just a few.

Just enter in the straight and narrow gate.

The Savior patiently waits.

Faith and repentance are all that's required.

It is your choice.   He waits.

The sun is setting and it's getting dark.

The Spirit beckons, please come home.

There's not much time.

Please don't wait.

Come home child before it's too late.

"Come to Me, all you who labor and are heavy laden, and I will give you rest."
(Matthew 11:28)

"The LORD has appeared of old to me, saying, "Yes, I have loved you with an everlasting love; therefore, with lovingkindness have I drawn you."
(Jeremiah 31:3)

"And I, if I be lifted up from the earth, will draw all people to Myself."
(John 12:32)

"Behold, I am coming quickly! Hold fast what you have, that no one may take your crown."
(Revelation 3:11)

"For you yourselves know perfectly that the day of the Lord so comes as a thief in the night."
(1 Thessalonians 5:2)

Only the Blood

It is only the blood

that can set me free.

Only the blood

that can give victory.

His precious blood

that can cleanse and set me free.

The place was Calvary

on a tree the Prince died for me.

A Prince and also a King

Jesus Christ is He.

"In Him we have redemption through His blood, the forgiveness of sins, according to the riches of His grace;"
(Ephesians 1:7)

"For whatever is born of God overcomes the world. And this is the victory that has overcome the world, our faith. Who is he who overcomes the world, but he who believes that Jesus is the Son of God? This is He that came by water and blood - Jesus Christ; not only by water, but by water and blood. And it is the Spirit who bears witness, because the Spirit is truth."
(1 John 5:4-6)

"But if we walk in the light as He is in the light, we have fellowship with one another, and the blood of Jesus Christ His Son cleanses us from all sin."
(1 John 1:7)

"For all have sinned and fall short of the glory of God, being justified freely by His grace through the redemption that is in Christ Jesus, whom God set forth as a propitiation by His blood, through faith, to demonstrate His righteousness, because in His forbearance God had passed over the sins that were previously committed,"
(Romans 3:23-25)

Let Me Not Forget

Let me not forget Dear Lord Jesus

of what You did for me,

so long ago at a place called Calvary.

There You would hang on that tree in my place,

it should have been me.

Oh, how Your precious blood did flow that day,

to wash all my guilt and sins away.

As You looked down upon the crowd that gathered,

many who didn't know or care of the burdens

and eventually the cross You would take up and bare.

In spite of their taunts and sneers,

You spoke these words so dear,

"Father forgive them, they now not what they do."

The love and mercy that You gave so freely,

I can't fully understand,

but You told me I don't have to understand

just hold onto Your hand and You will teach me.

That precious nailed scarred hand

that I hold onto each and every day,

is a reminder of the awful price that You chose to pay

for someone as unworthy as I.

You took my place that day.

You could have quit at any time,

but You chose to stay on a cross

that was meant for me,

so, I could be victorious and free.

I just want to thank You for all that you have done.

Oh, how precious You are, God's only Son!

"And He took bread, gave thanks and broke it, and gave it to them, saying, "This is My body which is given for you; do this in remembrance of Me."
(Luke 22:19)

"But the Helper, the Holy Spirit, whom the Father will send in My name, He will teach you all things, and bring to your remembrance all things that I said to you."

(John 14:26)

"So Pilate gave sentence that it should be as they requested."
(Luke 23:24)

"Now it was the third hour, and they crucified Him. And the inscription of His accusation was written above: "THE KING OF THE JEWS." With Him they crucify two robbers, one on His right and the other on His left. So the scripture was fulfilled which says, And He was numbered with the transgressors. And those who passed by blasphemed Him, wagging their heads and saying, "Aha! You who destroy the temple and build it in three days,"
(Mark 15:25-29)

The Stone's Been Rolled Away

The stone's been rolled away

from the entrance of the tomb.

The dark cold place that held

the body of my Savior,

the place of death that represents

sorrow and gloom.

Jesus gave the promise,

I'll rise again soon.

Yes, the stone's been rolled

from the entrance of the tomb.

On Easter morning

He came forth in resurrection power,

reigning King victorious over death,

hell and the grave.

Maybe you're in a prison

and there seems to be no way out;

just remember the stone's been rolled away,

Away from the entrance of the tomb.

"For He taught His disciples and said to them, "The Son of Man is being betrayed into the hands of men, and they will kill Him. And after that He is killed, He will rise the third day."
(Mark 9:31)

"Martha then said to Jesus, "Lord, if You had been here, my brother would not have died. Even now I know whatever You ask of God, God will give You." Jesus said to her, "Your brother will rise from the dead." Martha said to Him, "I know that he will rise again in the resurrection at the last day." Jesus said to her, "I am the resurrection and the life; the one who believes in Me will live, even if he dies, and everyone who lives and believes in Me will never die. Do you believe this?"

(John 11:21-26)

Let Faith Arise

Let faith arise.

Arise inside of me.

Dear Lord Jesus let me see,

see only thee.

The Author and Finisher of my faith.

When you speak to me

then my faith will rise,

arise inside of me.

"Looking unto Jesus, the author and finisher of our faith, who for the joy that was set before Him endured the cross, despising the shame, and has sat down at the right hand of the throne of God."
(Hebrews 12:2)

"Most assuredly, I say to you, the hour is coming, and now is, when the dead will hear the voice of the Son of God; and those who hear will live."
(John 5:25)

"So then faith comes by hearing, and hearing by the word of God."
(Romans 10:17)

"Then He arose and rebuked the wind, and said to the sea, "Peace, be still!" And the wind ceased and there was a great calm. But He said to them, "Why are you so fearful? How is it that you have no faith?"
(Mark 4:39-40)

Let faith arise speaks of a relationship, an intimacy between us and our Savior. We all should have and desire. This relationship can never be reached though religious efforts but only through us seeking Him with an open earnest longing heart. His voice means so much. There is such healing and strength in His words.

To Hear Your Voice

To hear Your voice means so much to me.

That still small voice

that I feel deep inside of my heart.

Your voice somehow makes everything alright,

Your voice turns my deep darkness

into pure light.

The words that You speak strengthen me

and serve as a healing balm to

my wounded soul.

Your voice is refreshing

as the crystal mountain streams that flow.

Your words are sweeter that honey, this I know.

"And after the earthquake a fire, but the Lord was not in the fire; and after the fire a still small voice."
(1 Kings 19:12)

"For He is our God, and we are the people of His pasture, and the sheep of His hand. Today, if you will hear His voice: Do not harden your hearts, as in the rebellion, as in the day of trial in the wilderness. When your fathers tested Me; they tried Me, though they saw My work."
(Psalms 95:7-9)

"Behold, I stand at the door and knock. If anyone hears My voice and opens the door, I will come in to him and dine with him, and he with Me."
(Revelation 3:20)

"Most assuredly, I say to you he who does not enter the sheepfold by the door, but climbs up some other way, the same is a thief and a robber. But he who enters by the door is the shepherd of the sheep. To him the doorkeeper opens, and the sheep hear his voice; and he calls his own sheep by name and leads them out. And when he brings out his own sheep, he goes before them; and the sheep follow him, for they know his voice."

(John 10:1-4)

God has much to say to us. Many believe that God does not speak to us. I know that He does speak to His own. It may not be in an audible voice, but we can hear it just the same. God's voice can calm the fiercest storm and is worth more than all the treasures on this Earth. How do I hear His voice? What moves the Heavenly Father is our genuine love for Him, not religion. He desires a relationship with us. Just be honest and open with Him and talk to Him like you would a friend. Be quiet before Him and listen. You will hear Him speak to your heart.

The Man

You were born amongst men to dwell,

in a lowly state, but yet a King.

A meek and humble person you are,

a true gentleman.

A wonderful person with so much love,

rich in mercy and so willing to give.

A servant to man You came to be,

to help and to save.

You're a close friend to anyone

who will let you be.

Someone who offers comfort in times of need.

Mankind's only hope,

the world's Savior.

You gave everything for me,

Your life so I could live and be free.

You made a way by bringing life

where there was death.

You are the man Christ Jesus,

I'm so thankful you came

and died for someone like me.

"For God so loved the world that He gave His only begotten Son, that whoever believes in Him should not perish but have everlasting life. For God did not send His Son into the world to condemn the world, but that the world through Him might be saved."

(John 3:16-17)

"Jesus said to him, "I am the way, the truth, and the life. No one comes to the Father except through Me."

(John 14:6)

All of Him

None of me, all of Him.

This is the way it must be

For He alone could make the way

He alone could pay the price

that was so high.

None of me, all of Him, it must be.

For if the world sees me,

all they see is a fallen man.

If they see Him in me,

then they see their Savior,

and for them to see Him, I must die.

It must be none of me and all of Him.

"He must increase, but I must decease."
(John 3:30)

"Now the Lord is the Spirit; and where the Spirit of the Lord is, there is liberty. But we all, with unveiled face beholding as in a mirror the glory of the Lord, are being transformed into the same image from glory to glory, just as by the Spirit of the Lord."
(2 Corinthians 3:17-18)

This poem is such a treasure to me. When I wrote it, I did not realize how special it was. I put it down in my journal, but unlike The Lighthouse, it really did not stand out. Later, I came across it in my journal and realized that it was yet another poem that the Lord had given me. I hope it truly blesses and finds you as it has me.

Our Daily Bread

Give us this day or daily bread.

Father God I pray.

For I need strength to journey through life's way.

Yes, the words of life that feed my soul,

heals all my hurt and makes me whole.

Yes, on the path of righteousness I choose to stay.

Just like the children of Israel so long ago,

You provided manna, just enough for each day.

When I wake in the morning,

you have so much to say.

If we will open our hearts when we kneel and pray,

with a song in my heart and praise on my lips

I stay close to your side, for without You

my feet would surely slip.

This bread that I'm talking about is Jesus Christ,

the Truth, the Life and the Way.

"Then Jesus said to them, "Most assuredly, I say unto you, Moses did not give you the bread from heaven, but My Father gives you the true bread from heaven. For the bread of God is He who comes down from heaven and gives life to the world. Then they said to Him, "Lord, give us this bread always."
(John 6:32-34)

"And Jesus said to them, "I am the bread of life. He who comes to Me shall never hunger, and he who believes in Me shall never thirst."
(John 6:35)

"And when you pray, do not use vain repetitions as the heathen do. For they think that they will be heard for their many words. Therefore do not be like them. For your Father knows the things you have need of before you ask Him. In this manner, therefore, pray:

Our Father who art in heaven,

Hallowed be thy name.

Thy kingdom come,

Thy will be done

On earth as it is in heaven.

Give us this day our daily bread.

And forgive us our debts,

As we forgive our debtors

And do not lead us not into temptation,

But deliver us from evil.

For Yours is the kingdom and the power

and the glory, forever.

Amen."

(Matthew 6:7-13)

Little Is Much When God Is In It

Little child, come and sit in your Father's lap.

You look so tired; He has rest for you.

You will be safe, go on and take your restful nap.

He loves you so He wants all of

His children to know.

You're the apple of His eye,

He has only the best for you dear child.

He doesn't see your sins or mistakes

because of the blood that covers you each day

as long as you stay by His side on the right path,

He promised He will lead and guide you

along your journey's path.

The promise was given to every child of God.

Just before Jesus ascended

to be with His Father in Glory,

not too many days from now

you will receive power from on high,

when the Holy Spirit shall come

to live inside of you and abide.

Never think or listen to the enemy

who will tell you a lie,

that your nothing, you don't matter,

and all of your religious talk is just chatter.

You might think your too small. What can I do?

But never forget of the power

and person that lives inside of you.

Just remember little David

who stood before the giant so big and tall.

Nobody thought that day Goliath would fall.

Although David was small,

his strength was great.

His strength wasn't in himself,

it was in the Lord the Rock.

The same strength and spirit

that was with David is now in you.

You might still think,

I'm too small what can I do?

Just remember little is much when God is in it.

You have been given the truth, now walk in it.

"So he answered and said to me: "This is the word of the LORD to Zerubbabel: Not by might, nor by power, but by My Spirit," says the LORD of hosts."
(Zechariah 4:6)

"God is my strength and power, and He makes my way perfect."
(2 Samuel 22:33)

"He gives power to the weak, and to those who have no might He increases strength."
(Isaiah 40:29)

"But you shall receive power when the Holy Spirit has come upon you; and you shall be witnesses to Me in Jerusalem, and in all Judea and Samaria, and to the end of the earth."
(Acts 1:8)

"For the eyes of the Lord run to and fro throughout the whole earth, to show Himself strong on behalf of those whose heart is loyal to Him..."
(2 Chronicles 16:9)

A Mother's Love

A Mother's love is one that is so strong and true.

Your love is one of sacrifice,

putting yourself last in all that you do.

You are a very special person indeed,

who is always there providing comfort

in times of heartache and need.

You have a special bond with your children

only a mother can know.

With every passing year, you watch your children grow,

and then one day you say goodbye and let them go.

God put a strength in you to carry out your mission,

of receiving His gift, teaching them of His love

and then giving them back.

Your duty is one of courage

and strength that is unsurpassed.

You wear a badge of honor that no one else can wear.

Your title is Mother, a very special person to be.

You make a house into a home

by filling it with Love, Happiness and Glee.

You strengthen your home by undergirding it with

Wisdom and Love that's from up above.

It's not hard to see that God gave you a special love

in your heart that is so strong and flows so free.

A Mother's Love is truly,

a special kind of love, indeed.

"Who can find a virtuous wife? For her worth is far above rubies."
(Proverbs 31:10)

"Strength and honor are her clothing; She shall rejoice in time to come."
(Proverbs 31:25)

"She watches over the ways of her household, and does not eat the bread of idleness."
(Proverbs 31:27)

"Many daughters have done well, but you excel them all. Charm is deceitful and beauty is passing, but a woman who fears the Lord, she shall be praised."
(Proverbs 31:29-30)

This poem is a tribute to the Christian soldiers we know as Mother. Mothers are special people who are courageous and strong, because they have great responsibilities facing them daily. Godly mothers are special people for all they do in the lives of their families. I hope that this poem is special to all the mothers who read it. Being a Mother is a great calling indeed.

Lady

Oh, lady how I love thee.

Oh, lady how I need thee.

When the night is cold and dark,

you're there to lift me up

and to show me that you care,

even when your day has been full of despair.

You show me love

when there is none sent your way

Your love never fails

to shine each and every day

You're a friend to me

surely the Lord has sent,

to help and to teach me,

about the love that He sent.

The love is Jesus Christ,

Yes, the same that flows

through your heart and touches me,

telling me we will never part.

Oh, lady how special you are,

to have the love of Jesus

and to see how He carried you this far.

I just want to say I love you lady,

and thank you for always being there for me,

never be afraid to let the love

that you have in your heart

flow so strong and so free.

"Who can find a virtuous wife? For her worth is far above rubies. The heart of her husband safely trusts her; so he will have no lack of grain. She does him good and not evil all the days of her life. She seeks wool and flax, and willingly works with her hands. She is like the merchant ships, she brings her food from afar. She also rises while it is yet night, and provides food for her household, and a portion for her maidservants. She considers a field and buys it; from her profits she plants a vineyard. She girds herself with strength and strengthens her arms. She perceives that her merchandise is good, and her lamp does not go out by night. She stretches out her hands to the distaff, and her hand holds the spindle. She extends her hand to the poor, yes, she

reaches out her hands to the needy. She is not afraid of snow for her household, for all her household is clothed with scarlet. She makes tapestry for herself; her clothing is fine linen and purple. Her husband is known in the gates, when he sits among the elders of the land. She makes linen garments and sell them, and supplies sashes for the merchants. Strength and honor are her clothing; She shall rejoice in time to come. She opens her mouth with wisdom, and on her tongue is the law of kindness. She watches over the ways of her household, and does not eat the bread of idleness. Her children rise up and call her blessed; her husband also, and he praises her: "Many daughters have done well, but you excel them all." Charm is deceitful and beauty is passing, but a woman who fears the Lord, she shall be praised. Give her of the fruit of her hands, and let her own works praise her in the gates."

(Proverbs 31:10-31)

Reflections

of

Truth

Each reflection of truth is a
word from the Lord that I hope
will bless and enrich your life.

As we love Jesus and He truly becomes our life, as we give our heart, our whole heart to Him then the darkness that hinders, blinds and hurts must flee because where there is light darkness cannot abide.

A child who loves his Father wants to be like his Father and strives to have his Father's approval.

"Therefore be imitators of God as dear children."

(Ephesians 5:1)

Jesus lives in the heart of everyone who genuinely loves because God is love and where the Father is the Son shall be also.

Life's greatest pursuits are Truth and Love one cannot exist without the other.

True beauty comes from within the heart as love flows like a fountain and brings forth a well spring of life.

A person listens with their ears, but one can only truly hear with their heart.

When our hearts are open to the Father and made pure with His love, it is then that we can truly hear and see the things that matter most in this life.

Instead of trying to make the Father's word line up with our lives, we should line up our lives with the Father's word.

"Behold, I stand at the door and knock. If anyone hears My voice and opens the door, I will come in to him and dine with him, and he with Me."

(Revelation 3:20)

Faith and Love are the two avenues in which God moves.

Love is great; Love can mend the broken heart and is able to heal the sin sick heart. Love can open prison doors, as well as blinded eyes. Love can change a world; Love can do all things for God is love.

"But seek first the kingdom of God and His righteousness, and all these things shall be added to you." (Matthew 6:33)

We should spend time alone with God every day.

God is bigger than any problem we might have and is able to turn any bad situation around.

A person whose life is lived unto God will always be remembered.

A Christian's life should be lived to the glory of God. Everything that we do, say, and are should be pondered because we either bring glory to Him or shame.

God's promises are so great and so true.

One is truly rich if they are blessed with the Fruit of God's spirit.

Intimacy is when two people open their hearts to share love and through this becomes one.

There is one word that best describes the Cross...Love.

I have pondered the footsteps of my path on this journey that I take. I have come to the full conclusion that no good thing dwells in the heart of man apart from God. The only good and righteous things man can know are from God. By man having faith in Jesus and His finished work then His gifts we can know and have.

God our Father does not see us as others do or often as we see ourselves. He sees us as having great potential and as His children, a peculiar treasure. He looks upon us with eyes of love; in His word He says we are being molded, shaped, and formed into His image by the cleansing of His blood, the truth of his word and the power of his spirit.

It is more blessed to give than to receive, because when we give from our hearts selflessly then God can bless greatly.

A better place this world would be if everyone made the choice to serve one person in need every day.

If I have lived my life in the gifts the Lord has chosen for me and used them to show His love to others, then I am truly a success. If I have wasted my gifts on vanity and worldly pursuits for myself then I have utterly failed.

If we are to shine with God's marvelous light, we must allow Him to remove from us that which is not like Him. It may seem too costly at the time, but if we make the decision to live for Him, we will find that the thing that has been taken away from us that we once held so dear has been replaced by something much grander and eternal.

When we do good to others what we are doing is making deposits in Heaven when we do good or evil, we are doing it to God. Every man should ponder his ways to make sure his life is one that is pleasing to God.

God's love is a love that will not let us go...love that will not let me go.

To store up heavenly treasures. One who does right has the promise that he will be blessed of God. The same who chooses to do evil, he will not be blessed but cursed. Forgiveness and healing are always given to people who confess and turn from their wicked ways.

A caterpillar is not very pretty or graceful just as we are not before we come to Christ. In time however, the caterpillar undergoes a change as it feeds on the green leaves and its body is nourished just as we cannot be unchanged as we feed on God's word and let its magnificent truth change our hearts. When the caterpillar has been changed the force that once held it earthbound no longer can hold it down. It now is in its intended state, a butterfly, that is so beautiful and free to ride upon the wind beneath its wings. When we as Christian's allow God to change us well find that the chains of sin that once held us down can no longer hold us in bondage because God's truth has broken them.

Man was created to love and to fellowship with his maker. Due to his disobedience, man lost fellowship with God and the ability to love without interruption. Man now introduced wickedness into his heart by rebelling against God.

The Father being full of love and rich in grace and mercy gave man the promise of hope that man could be free, free once and for all to love and live forever. All man would have to do is believe in His Son, Jesus Christ as the sacrifice for man's rebellion.

Jesus

Our

Everything

In the Book of Genesis, He is the One Promised that would crush the head of the serpent.

In the Book of Exodus, He is the Passover Lamb.

In the Book of Leviticus, He is the Acceptable Sacrifice.

In the Book of Numbers, He is the Cloud by Day and the Fire by Night.

In the Book of Deuteronomy, He is the Law Fulfilled.

In the Book of Joshua, He is the Way where there seems to be no way.

In the Book of Judges, He is our Strength.

In the Book of Ruth, He is the Promise of Redemption.

In the Book of 1 Samuel, He is the Lord of Hosts.

In the Book of 2 Samuel, He is the One who will defeat all of your enemies.

In the Book of 1 Kings, He is the Still Small Voice.

In the Book of 2 Kings, He is the Bread of Life.

In the Book of 1 Chronicles, He is Ours.

In the Book of 2 Chronicles, He is the Place for us to dwell forever.

In the Book of Ezra, He is the Right Way for us.

In the Book of Nehemiah, He is the Light.

In the Book of Esther, He is our Victory.

In the Book of Job, He is our Mediator.

In the Book of Psalms, He is the Rock of our Salvation.

In the Book of Proverbs, He is the Hope of the Righteous.

In the Book of Ecclesiastes, He is our Wisdom.

In the Book of Solomon, He is the Banner over us.

In the Book of Isaiah, He is Emmanuel meaning God With Us.

In the Book of Jeremiah, He is the Better Way.

In the Book of Lamentations, He is our Portion.

In the Book of Ezekiel, He is the Wheel in the Middle of the Wheel.

In the Book of Daniel, He is the Fourth Man in the Fire.

In the Book of Hosea, He is the Lilly of the Valley.

In the Book of Joel, He is the one who Restores.

In the Book of Amos, He is the Promise.

In the Book of Obadiah, He is our Victory.

In the Book of Jonah, He is Our Deliverer.

In the Book of Micah, He is our Promised King.

In the Book of Nahum, He is our Stronghold in the Day of Trouble.

In the Book of Habakkuk, He is our Salvation.

In the Book of Zephaniah, He is our Reigning King.

In the Book of Haggai, He is the One Who Has Chosen Us.

In the Book of Zechariah, He is our Chief Cornerstone.

In the Book of Malachi, He is the Lamb of God that taketh away the sins of the world.

In the Book of Matthew, He is the Bread of Life.

In the Book of Mark, He is our Healer.

In the Book of Luke, He is the one who Calms the Storms.

In the Book of John, He is the Light of the World.

In the Book of Acts, He is the One who Baptizes with the Holy Spirit.

In the Book of Romans, He is our Victory.

In the Book of 1 Corinthians,
He is the wisdom of God.

In the Book of 2 Corinthians,
He is our Strength.

In the Book of Galatians, He is
our Liberator.

In the Book of Ephesians, He is the Fullness of God.

In the Book of Philippians, He is our Confidence.

In the Book of Colossians, He is our Redeemer.

In the Book of 1 Thessalonians,

He is the one who will Descend

from Heaven with a shout.

In the Book of 2 Thessalonians,

He is our Lord.

In the book of 1 Timothy, He is

the man Christ Jesus.

In the Book of 2 Timothy, He is our Righteous Judge.

In the Book of Titus, He is our Blessed Hope.

In the Book of Philemon, He is our Joy.

In the Book of Hebrews, He is our High Priest.

In the Book of James, He is the overseer of Our Souls.

In the Book of 1 Peter, He is the Chief Corner Stone.

In the Book of 2 Peter, He is
the Light that shines in a dark
place.

In the Book of 1 John, He is
Eternal Life.

In the Book of 2 John, He is our
Truth.

In the Book of 3 John, He is Head of the Church.

In the Book of Jude, He is the one who is able to keep us from stumbling.

In the Book of Revelation, He is the Root and Offspring of David, the Bright and Morning Star. He is the Lamb on the Throne. He is the one that will stick closer than a brother.

He is the one who cannot fail, the one who is more than able, the Mighty One of Israel, King of Kings, Lord of Lords, the fairest of ten thousand, The Atonement.

Our Lord Jesus Christ!

In Loving Memory Of

Farrell J. Curry, Sr.

Rosemary Curry

I will see you again as we walk
the streets of gold with the Savior.

Special Acknowledgments

I would like to thank first and foremost my Heavenly Father who has done so much for me by sending His Son to die for me!

Thank you to my family for giving me the support and encouragement to keep going.

Thank you to Michelle, My Lady, for your tireless efforts and many hours of editing. You helped in making my dream and God's gift a reality.

I hope that you enjoyed reading The Lighthouse. If, during your reading, you found that you desire a relationship with God – pray the following prayer and accept Jesus into your heart.

"Lord Jesus, I confess my sins and ask for your forgiveness. Please come into my heart as my Lord and Savior. Take complete control of my life and help me to walk in Your footsteps daily by the power of the Holy Spirit. Thank you, Lord, for saving me and for answering my prayer. In Jesus' name. Amen."

(The Prayer of Salvation – National Association of American Veterans, Inc.)

"For He made Him who knew no sin to be sin for us, that we might become the righteousness of God in Him."
(Corinthians 5:21)

"These things I have written to you who believe in the name of the Son of God, in order that you may know that you have eternal life."
(1 John 5:13)

"For by the grace you have been saved through faith, and that not of yourselves; it is the gift of God, not of works, lest anyone should boast."
(Ephesians 2:8-9)

About the Author

After the death of my father at the tender age of 6, I knew the Lord had His hand on my life as my Heavenly Father.

I became a student of the Bible in my youth and my passion for writing I discovered in college.

God has continued to prove His undying love for me again and again.

I have suffered much in my life, some of which was my fault and some not. One of the most important lessons I have learned is that God is bigger than any trial that we may be in and that His love and mercy for us is undying.

At the time that God gave me The Lighthouse, I was in a terrible place in my life, but the Lord chose me to write His poems.

I have a close personal relationship with God once again in my life. I hope that this book of poetry helps you find a closer relationship with the Lord and blesses you today, tomorrow and all the days that follow.

God bless you!

EJC

Farrell J. Curry, Jr. was born in

Plaquemine, Louisiana, across the

Mississippi River from Baton Rouge.

Visit me at – EJCProductions.com